STARTERS

Bread

Saviour Pirotta

Text copyright © Saviour Pirotta 2004

Language consultant: Andrew Burrell
Subject consultant: Carol Ballard
Design: Perry Tate Design
Picture research: Glass Onion Pictures

Published in Great Britain in 2004
by Hodder Wayland, an imprint of
Hodder Children's Books

This paperback edition published in 2007 by Wayland,
an imprint of Hachette Children's books
Reprinted in 2007, 2008 and 2009 (twice)

The right of Saviour Pirotta to be identified as the author of this Work has been
asserted by her in accordance with the Copyright, Designs and Patents Act 1988

The publishers would like to thank the following for allowing us to reproduce their
pictures in this book: Angela Hampton Family Life Picture Library; title page, 17
(bottom right) / Cephas; 4 / Corbis; 11 (bottom), 12 (bottom), 22 (bottom), 23 (top) /
Foodpix; 12, 23 (bottom) / Getty; 5 (bottom), 7, 8, 10 / Wayland Picture Library;
contents page, 9, 17 (top left and right, bottom left), 18, 19, 20 (top), 21 (top) /
Stockfood; cover; 6, 7, 11 (top), 12 (top), 13, 15 (top), 20 (bottom), 22 (top) / Topham
Picturepoint; 15 (bottom), 16 (Chapman) / Travel Ink; 21 (bottom)

A catalogue record for this book is available from the British Library.

ISBN: 978 0 7502 4550 0

Printed and bound in China

Wayland
338 Euston Road, London NW1 3BH
Wayland is a division of Hachette Children's Books,
an Hachette UK Company.
www.hachette.co.uk

Contents

Bread, delicious bread

Bread! How could we live without it?

We toast it for breakfast in the morning.

Egg and toast soldiers make a tasty breakfast!

We use it for
making sandwiches
at lunchtime.

Sandwiches can have
all kinds of delicious
fillings.

We might DIP it in
soup, or toast it
with cheese for
supper.

Most bread is made from grain, the seed-like fruit of special grasses. You can make bread from rye, millet, oats, corn or wheat.

These crispbreads are made from different types of grain.

Rye bread is very popular in Northern Europe.

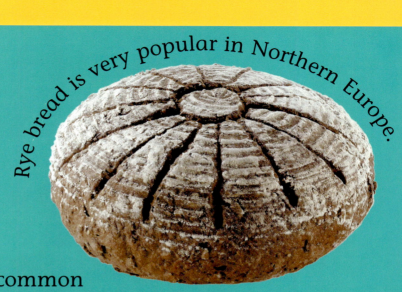

But the most common bread is made from wheat.

Farmers grow wheat in **enormous** fields. When it's ripe, they collect the grain with a special machine called a combine harvester.

This wheat is ready for harvest.

The harvester cuts the wheat with sharp, turning blades. It also sorts the grain from the stalks, which it drops back onto the ground.

The combine harvester pours the grain into the trailer.

At the mill

The farmer sends his grain to the flourmill. There it's piled up HIGH, ready to be cleaned again and again to make sure there is no dirt in it.

The clean grains are then passed through metal rollers, which CRUSH and grind them into flour.

The fresh new flour is collected in large sacks.

From the mill, the flour goes to the bakery. The baker mixes it with water, yeast, and a little sugar and salt.

The baker kneads the mixture.

The yeast in the dough makes it grow **bigger**. The baker cuts it into pieces to make loaves.

The loaves are baked in the oven until they are crisp and ready to eat. Yum! Yum!

Mmmm, that bread smells delicious!

The bread factory

At some big bakeries, the bread is made by machines. First the dough is made in **GIANT** mixers.

Then another machine splits it into loaves and rolls.

These rolls are ready for the oven.

The bread travels slowly through the oven.
When it comes out the other side,
the bread is baked. It's ready
to be sliced and packed.

Wrapping the bread
keeps it fresh.

Before long, the bread is in the shops for people to buy. **Mmm**, the smell of fresh loaves draws people to the bread counter.

This man is buying a French stick.

There are so many different kinds to choose from. **Long** and crusty. *Round* and soft. Square tin loaves. Sliced loaves in packets. White bread, brown bread and wholemeal!

foccacia

bagel

It makes your tummy rumble with hunger.

croissant

wholemeal loaf

Bread is not
only delicious;
it is also very good
for you. Bread gives
you energy. It helps
keep you healthy.

Bread helps you
to run, jump
and play.

Bread also contains fibre. This can help your blood to flow around your body. It also helps to push waste through it.

For extra fibre, wholemeal bread is best.

People all over the world enjoy bread.

In India they eat round nan bread and chapattis with curry and rice.

In Turkey they stuff pockets of pitta bread with cheese and salad, or with slices of meat.

In Mexico they wrap spicy meat, beans and vegetables in tortillas.

Pizza is a **F L A T** bread from Italy, covered in different toppings. It's enjoyed by people in many countries.

Pizza is delicious!

Celebrate!

Bread helps us celebrate too. In some countries, people eat a special Easter bread. It's made in beautiful shapes, and decorated with eggs or nuts and fruit.

Jewish people celebrate the festival of Passover with special, flat bread.

Christmas bread can come in special shapes. It sometimes has icing and fruit on top.

No wonder bread is one of the most popular foods in the world.

Glossary and index